Breaking Through The Darkness

John McConnel

Breaking Through The Darkness

How to defeat depression, anxiety and stress
– a spiritual perspective

Breaking Through The Darkness
How to defeat depression, anxiety and stress – a spiritual perspective
John McConnel

ISBN 978-1-78972-992-4

Website: http://www.stresslesstraining.co.uk

Email: info@stresslesstraining.co.uk

Book cover design: Shaan Sampat

Interior design: http://babental.com

Disclaimer: The tools and insights in this book are offered as suggestions, which may help you. They are not intended as a substitute for psychiatric and/or medical help, counselling or other forms of treatment but as an additional support.

To all travellers of the Night
and the One who is guiding us
to the Light

The Guest House

This being human is a guest house.

Every morning a new arrival.

A joy, a depression, a meanness,
some momentary awareness
comes as an unexpected visitor.

Welcome and entertain them all!

Even if they are a crowd of sorrows,
who violently sweep your house
empty of its furniture,
still, treat each guest honorably.

He may be clearing you out
for some new delight.
The dark thought, the shame, the malice.

Meet them at the door laughing
and invite them in.

Be grateful for whatever comes
because each has been sent
as a guide from beyond.

Jellaludin Rumi
Translation by Coleman Barks

CONTENTS

PREFACE

THIS BOOK IS FOR ANYONE who feels anxious, stressed, unhappy or depressed.

It is intended to be a simple practical guide to dealing with depression and other negative states of mind from a spiritual perspective.

It is based on the understanding that, at the heart of every human being, there is a core of powerful, positive spiritual energy. Whether we realise it or not, we are by nature beings of peace, love and joy. Such qualities are part of our original spiritual DNA.

Over time, journeying through this complicated and confusing world, we have lost our way. Our truth has become suppressed and submerged under a deluge of distractions, distortions and distressing life events. Songs of innocence have been replaced by songs of experience[1]. By remembering who we really are and re-connecting with the Light, magic happens. Depression changes from a curse into a blessing, a gift that can lead to self-transformation.

---

[1]The title of two poems written by William Blake.

This book is divided into two parts.

PART 1: provides an understanding of depression and a spiritual framework to enable us to climb out of the bog of depression and return to our original state of contentment. It includes a four-step process, which can be summarised as follows:

1. Understanding the Mind/Body Connection

2. Thinking Positively

3. Being Soul Conscious

4. Connecting With The Light.

Each step offers food for thought and there are reflective experiments to consolidate the learning and provide an opportunity to tune in to our own inner wisdom.

PART 2: consists of a series of reflective experiments designed to reinforce the theory with practical experiences that will, hopefully, help us to break through the darkness into the Light of love, peace and hope.

The fact that you are reading this book is a sign that you are well on the road to understanding and transforming yourself.

Please note that all the tools and insights that follow are offered as suggestions, which may help you. *They are not intended as a substitute for psychiatric and/or medical help, counselling or other forms of treatment but as an additional support.*

INTRODUCTION

DEPRESSION IS A WORLDWIDE PHENOMENON. It covers a range of mental and emotional states, including anxiety, worry, low mood, insecurity, hopelessness and despair. It is something that affects us all, to a greater or lesser extent, at some stage or other in our life. It is no respecter of age, gender, ethnicity, or social position. Even children may experience it.

This perhaps is not surprising as we are living in an age of unprecedented global, social, economic, political and environmental change. Some scientists are even talking about the end of the world as we know it within the next few years! Consequently, many people are feeling insecure, fragile, confused and under intense pressure in some, or all, areas of their life. These external pressures are often exacerbated by feelings of anger resulting from negative conditioning and/or traumatic experiences involving the people who were expected to provide us with love and support during our early years.

Most people shy away from acknowledging these problems and so rarely seek help. Those who do, are offered a variety of therapies, which may include counselling, CBT (cognitive behavioural therapy), medication, psychiatry, rehabiltiation or hospitalisation. All of these, in one way or another, may help and indeed form an important part of dealing with a complex range of conditions or 'states of being'. However, the spiritual aspect and its role in mental health disorders is often overlooked or neglected.

In my opinion, it helps immensely if we can rediscover our spirit and reclaim our peace of mind. *This key understanding is the backbone of this book.*

In what follows, I will share my own understanding about depression based on my experience and study. I am not a doctor, therapist, or expert on the subject. However, I have worked as a prison governor, social worker and stress management trainer and dealt with many depressed and stressed people in my life, including myself! I have also been studying and teaching Raja Yoga meditation for nearly 30 years.[2]

I would like to offer some food for thought and some spiritual tools and techniques that I have found helpful, in the hope that they will help you and others too.

---

[2]Raja yoga is a method of open-eyed meditation in which we connect with our higher self and the Divine and experience inner peace and happiness.

PART 1:
Depression & Spirituality

"The best thing for being sad," replied Merlin, beginning to puff and blow, "is to learn something. That's the only thing that never fails".

T.H. White, *The Once and Future King*

The spiritual path is like a school. Not a regular school where you learn ordinary skills, but a spiritual school where you learn the skills of spirit – like how to remove flaws in your character, or how to remain unaffected by the negative influences around you.

Dadi Janki, *Companion of God*

WHAT IS DEPRESSION?

Depression is 'a mental condition characterised by feelings of severe despondency and dejection, typically also with feelings of inadequacy and guilt' (Oxford English Dictionary).

According to the World Health Organisation[3]

- Depression is a common mental disorder. Globally, more than 264 million people of all ages suffer from depression.
- Depression is the leading cause of disability worldwide and is a major contributor to the overall global burden of disease.
- More women are affected by depression than men.
- At its worst, depression can lead to suicide. Close to 800,000 people in the world take their own life every year. Suicide is the second leading cause of death in 15-29 year olds.

Trillions of dollars are spent annually on antidepressants to dull the pain, suppress the symptoms and enable people to at least go through the motions of living a normal life, whatever that may be.

---

[3]World Health Organisation Website: Fact Sheet on Depression, December 2019

According to the figures obtained from the National Health Service Business Services Authority[4]:

- One in six 18 to 64-year-olds in England were prescribed antidepressants at some point in 2017/18, rising to one in five among those aged 65 and over.
- 4 million people were taking antidepressants on a long-term basis.
- Twice as many women as men were prescribed antidepressants in all age groups.

[4]See article in The Guardian dated 10 August 2018

THE SIGNS OF DEPRESSION

Feelings of depression vary in duration and intensity. The challenges of life are such that most of us at some time in our life feel anxious, insecure, low in spirit, inadequate, disheartened, demoralized or hopeless. Often these feelings can be reduced or removed with the support and company of other people, or a good night's sleep, the relaxing effect of a trip to the gym, or a walk in the park.

Sometimes the feelings and the mood get deeper and darker and we enter a space from which we feel there is no return. We become a different person, a shadow of our former happy self. In these circumstances, depression is experienced as a very distressing and debilitating state of being.

Depression drains our energy, paralyses our willpower, spoils our relationships and reduces the quality of our life to ashes. It is often described as like living under a dark cloud, being trapped in a black hole or a tunnel with no light at the end, or a bottomless pit. Lost and lonely, we feel so heavy that we can hardly drag ourselves out of bed and when we finally do succeed, we can barely raise our head, open our mouth or move our leaden feet. Battered and worn down by the efforts of living, like a tortoise under siege, we withdraw and live in a mental hell, feeling hopeless and helpless, unlovable and unreachable, in the world but not of the world.

At one stage in my life, years ago when going through a very challenging period, suicide felt like an attractive option. This was the start of a long journey of self study which involved reading lots of self-help books, attending different personal development courses and workshops as well as exploring Buddhism, the Quakers and some aspects of Hinduism. I found the spiritual approach of the Brahma Kumaris World Spiritual University[5] to be particularly beneficial, and in fact, I still study with them.

---

[5]The Brahma Kumaris is a world-wide spiritual organisation dedicated to achieving world peace through personal growth and transformation. See Appendix 1 for further information.

DEPRESSION — A SPIRITUAL CRISIS?

I have come to the conclusion that some aspects of depression are less of a mental/physical condition and more of a spiritual crisis, which has been medicalised. It can be a form of spiritual dis-ease/spiritual amnesia, or, put another way, an existential crisis.

Who am I?

There must be more to life than this (whatever 'this' might be)? What's it all about?

Why do I feel so anxious and insecure all the time?

Why am I always so angry and confused?

Not knowing the answers to such questions, in my experience, lies at the heart of many types of depression.

Such questions are not new. For centuries people have experienced what is often referred to as 'the dark night of the soul'. Many have spent years desperately seeking solace through the study of religious texts or books on philosophy. Others have journeyed within, seeking answers through contemplation, meditation, prayer, pilgrimages or communing with nature.

What is new in our era is the rapid global decline of organised religion and the parallel rise of scientific rationalism and mass consumerism. The worship of gods, saints and gurus has been replaced by the religion of science and the cult of celebrity with its emphasis on good looks and material success. For some scientists and social commentators, human beings are little more than an advanced type of ape or chimpanzee that has evolved over millennia, ruled by its brain and instinct for survival. Just like other animals we come and go and that's it! Here today and gone tomorrow.

The wisdom and insights of spirituality and religion gathered over thousands of years are often brushed aside. There is no longer an agreed common understanding or language through which we can talk about the deeper aspects of ourselves and the need to belong and live with others in a state of peace, harmony and common purpose.

We have thrown the baby out with the bath water and are left floundering in a state of limbo, not knowing where to turn or what to do.

This situation has been made more challenging by the profound psychological legacy of those religions that tend to emphasise the sinful nature of humanity. Consequently, from an early age we can be made to feel 'not good enough' and are controlled through a mixture of fear (of rejection and disapproval) and punishment. The result? Low self-esteem and a lack of confidence in ourselves.

In most societies, our essentially good nature has been suppressed by a collective barrage of criticism, complaint, blame, judgments and comparison from parents, teachers and significant others. This has been fuelled by the media and an advertising industry, which plays on our insecurities and anxieties and does its best to create dissatisfaction and discontent in our lives.

To this can be added the effects of adverse childhood experiences[6] and other traumas and losses that have occurred in our life.

A root cause of many types of depression is suppressed anger. Anger with ourselves for not being good enough, or for being unable to express our feelings towards parents, teachers or other authority figures and significant people in our life, whom we consider to have hurt us in some way.

This double whammy of being angry with ourselves and being unable to express our anger towards others, sets in motion a constantly spinning cycle of inadequacy, guilt, shame and blame and condemns us to a sad and lonely life.

How do we rectify this unhappy situation and start to shift the darkness? Through using our spiritual intelligence.

---

[6]Research into Adverse Childhood Experiences (ACE) indicates that there is a strong link between such experiences and depression. See Appendix 2.

SPIRITUAL INTELLIGENCE

Wherever there is darkness, let there be light.

Nobody likes being kept in the dark, whether it's the physical darkness of being in a room in which there is no light, or the darkness of ignorance where we are unaware of what is really going on in our world. Darkness creates fear and tension both within us and in our relationships with others.

Light brings relief and hope. We can see things more clearly and make informed decisions as to where to go and what to do.

This book is about shedding some spiritual light on ways to break through the darkness of depression. Its foundation is what is sometimes referred to as the ultimate intelligence i.e. *spiritual intelligence.*

WHAT IS SPIRITUAL INTELLIGENCE?

Spiritual intelligence is about understanding that each of us is a unique human *being* and not just a highly evolved animal. This being is a form of conscious energy connected to but separate from the body. It is referred to in a variety of ways e.g. soul, spirit, higher self and atma.

Each of us is a soul and we have a body.

The soul is the source of our conscience, intuition, will power, qualities, values and virtues - the body is the instrument/vehicle/costume through which it expresses itself.

The analogy of the driver and the car is often used to illustrate this. The driver is separate from the car. S/he enters the car and, after turning on the engine, controls the movements of the car on its journey from A to B. However much we might like or love our car, we do not consider ourselves to be the car. The same cannot be said of our relationship with our body. Often we get confused and think we are our body. This *'body consciousness'* lies at the heart of many of our difficulties.

Brahma Kumaris and many others[7] believe in the 'original goodness' of all souls rather than the idea of 'original sin'. Each soul when it first enters a body is pure and powerful and its nature is one of peace, love and joy. Over time it may lose its power and purity and become 'sinful'. As someone who was brought up to consider myself to be a 'sinner' and had to beg for God's forgiveness, I find this approach to be a blessed and reassuring relief. It also makes a lot of sense.

Spirituality does not necessarily involve a belief in a god, or a particular religion. It does involve recognising, appreciating, nurturing and empowering the inner being and looking beneath the surface of life for its deeper meaning and purpose.

Spirituality also holds that we are eternal powerful beings who create our own life and destiny. The life we are currently living

---

[7]Many mystics, poets and spiritual teachers speak of the light and the love that lies within each human being, including Rumi, Echart Tolle, Marianne Williamson, Wayne Dwyer, Byron Katie, Brandon Bays, Louise L Hay to name but a few.

is a product of our own thoughts, words and actions, the result of all the many decisions we have made along the way.

We are not born depressed, anxious or stressed. We become depressed, anxious or stressed.

Over time we lose our happiness and peace due to various life experiences.

Accepting this truth and taking responsibility for our life, including our negative state of mind, is essential if we wish to start breaking through the darkness.

If you're feeling very depressed, anxious or stressed at the moment, this may be the last thing that you want to hear! On the other hand, it might be the lifeline you have been looking for.

FOUR STEPS TO SHIFT THE DARKNESS

If I am a truly knowledgeable soul,
I will be skillful in the things of the spirit.
I will be centered successfully in my spiritual identity.
I will be free from the influence of my past.
There will only be peace and happiness within.

Dadi Janki, *Companion of God*

WHEN WE REMEMBER AND RECONNECT with our original eternal goodness, a shift happens. We feel better in ourselves and we are able to dis-identify from the feelings of depression in the same way as the driver dis-identifies from the car. At the same time we open ourselves to a whole new world of possibilities.

The following four steps are designed to facilitate this process. They are four interconnected and powerful ways of thinking and being which, together, can offer real hope for breaking through the darkness of depression, anxiety and stress.

STEP 1. UNDERSTAND THE MIND/BODY CONNECTION

The mind and body are not separate units,
but one integrated system.
How we act and what we think, eat,
and feel are all related to our health.

Bernie Siegel

THERE IS A STRONG CONNECTION between the mind and body: whatever we think in our mind will affect our body. For example, when we get upset about anything the body automatically triggers what is called the 'fight or flight' reaction - adrenaline is pumped round the body, cortisol is injected into the bloodstream, the muscles tense, the breath becomes more shallow, the heart beats faster and many toxic chemicals are released into the body.

This reaction is designed to help us deal with perceived situations of danger. Originally it was developed in the days when we lived in nature, wild animals roamed the earth and we faced physical dangers, which required an emergency supply of extra strength and energy. It was not intended to become our general *modus operandi.*

In our day and age the 'fight and flight' response has become associated with mundane, everyday occurrences. For example, it is a form of madness that many of us no longer make a distinction in our mind between a tiger entering the room and the train being late, or someone shouting at us down the phone! We are constantly getting upset, frustrated, or angry, triggering the 'fight or flight' reaction many times each day.

In these circumstances, it is not surprising that our immune system gets overwhelmed and we become susceptible to a variety medical conditions such as high blood pressure, heart disease, eczema, musculoskeletal disorders, cancer and, of course, depression.

When we are in a good mood and feel happy, endorphins, serotonin and other 'feel good' chemicals are generated in the brain. We feel peaceful and calm, the world is our friend and we enjoy being alone or in the company of other people. This is the way we are meant to be. This is why we like to walk in nature, go on holiday to 'get away from it all', enjoy a drink with friends, or take part in a sport.

The ideal state of both the body and the mind is one of peace.

When we are calm and relaxed the body feels good and the mind is able to see things clearly and make more effective decisions. We feel more in control of our life. And we feel happy.

If we wish to shift the darkness of depression, it is important to develop the art of being peaceful.

To do this we need to take control of the body as well as the mind.

How?

By doing simple relaxation exercises such as diaphragm breathing, progressive muscle relaxation and positive visualisation[8], as well as stretching exercises and gentle movements.

If we were to get up 20 minutes earlier each day and take control of our mind and body in these ways we would feel more in control of our life and have more positive energy to face the day.

Here are some other suggestions to help you improve your body and your mind and so help prevent or ameliorate the effects of depression.

---

[8]For examples, see the 'I Breathe', 'I Relax' and 'I Am Well' reflective experiments in Part 2.

BE MINDFUL

Mindfulness is a powerful technique for calming the mind and the body. By taking time to sit and observe our breath, the experience of our senses, the feelings in our body and our emotions, we are able to become fully present in the moment. In this state, when there are no thoughts of the past or the future, depression temporarily disappears. Mindfulness can be practiced anywhere, at any time and is very effective. Hence, its massive worldwide appeal.

EXPERIMENT

- Find a quite space
- Switch off your phone and other electronic distractions and sit comfortably in a chair or on the floor
- Breath slowly, deeply and gently into your diaphragm through your nose
- Exhale through your mouth
- Observe the air as it enters and leaves the body
- Become aware of your body
- Scan your body starting with your feet

- Notice the sensations and movements in your toes and feet as they rest on the floor
- Then take your attention to your calf muscles and thighs
- Buttocks
- Stomach
- Chest area and all your internal organs
- Back
- Shoulders
- Neck
- Throat, tongue, jaw, eyes, scalp
- Observe, without judgement, any movement, itches, tension, or other messages being transmitted from either inside or outside your body
- Notice the support you are receiving from the chair and the floor on which it is placed
- With your head still, move your eyes to the left, right, up and down and notice everything around you
- With your ears, notice all the sounds around you
- Turning your attention inwards notice and observe the thoughts in your mind. Let them pass like clouds

- Notice your emotions. Are you feeling sad, lonely, happy or calm?
- Now bring your attention back into the room and start to slowly move your body and become more generally aware of your surroundings
- Check how you are feeling hopefully more alert and peaceful.

SHARPEN YOUR SAW

Stephen Covey in his book, 'The 7 Habits Of Highly Effective People' talks about 'sharpening the saw' and 'the four dimensions of renewal'. Just as it is much harder to saw wood with a blunt saw, so it takes a lot more effort to live effectively if we do not pay attention to the physical, mental, social/ emotional and spiritual aspects of ourselves.

'We need to 'exercise all four dimensions of our nature, regularly and consistently in wise and balanced ways'.

One of the reasons we may get or be depressed is that the saw of our life has got blunt or worn out through excessive use and is no longer working effectively. Alternatively, lack of use of the saw of our life can also cause depression. If we do not have the energy, will or enthusiasm to express the different aspects of ourselves, they can fall into abeyance. 'Use it or lose it' as the saying goes.

Without going into too much detail as this book is mainly concerned with the spiritual aspects of depression, there are a number of things we can do to improve the quality of our life and prevent or reduce the likelihood of becoming depressed or stressed.

Physical Sharpening

Get Into Sport and Other Activities

Taking part in a sport or some other form of physical activity[9] is a great way to relieve depression. It is for this reason that some doctors prescribe free access to the local sports centre for patients who are depressed. Sporting activities and hobbies or interests give us an opportunity to focus on something other than our mental condition and also meet people and talk about other things.

When the activity becomes a regular part of our routine, it gives us a reason to get out of bed in the morning.

PAUSE FOR THOUGHT

- Write down the physical activities, hobbies or interests you already enjoy and three others you would like to do if you could.
- How do they, or how could they, improve the quality of your life?

---

[9]For example knitting groups are taking off in a big way all over the world. Knitting helps focus the mind, relieves tension and reduces social isolation.

Eat and Drink Well

We are what we eat and drink - both the mind and the body are affected by what we consume. When depressed or stressed, we often resort to 'comfort foods' such as biscuits, cakes and chocolate, or dull our inner pain through alcohol and other mind-altering substances. Such relief is only temporary and, in the long run, it can compound our problems by creating dependency, addiction and serious health challenges such as obesity, diabetes and heart or liver conditions.

Along with comfort foods, many dieticians recommend that we reduce or eliminate our consumption of what are often called the 'four white poisons' i.e. processed sugar, salt, flour and rice. Such foods have little nutritional value and generate a lot of acid in the body (cancer cells thrive in acid).

Ideally we also need to avoid animal products, not just for the benefit of animals and the environment but also for our own peace of mind. As animals are killed in a state of fear and tension, their flesh is filled with adrenaline, other toxic chemicals and negative vibrations which, when consumed by humans, do actually affect our mind as well as our body.

With regards drink, it is healthier to drink water rather than alcohol and caffeine-based drinks. The UK's National Health Service advises drinking between six to eight glasses of fluid a day, including lower fat milk, sugar-free drinks, tea and coffee.

When considering these issues it is important not to feel guilty or bad about our struggle with food and drink. We are on a journey of self-discovery.

When we understand and deal with the underlying issues that drive our unhealthy consumption choices, we will find the strength and determination to look after ourselves in better ways.

In the meantime, we can be kind to ourselves and take small steps in the right direction. For example by putting one less spoon of white sugar in each cup of tea or coffee we drink. Gradually, over time, we will build up our confidence and self-discipline and resist the constant bombardments of the advertising industry.

PAUSE FOR THOUGHT

- Reflect on your diet.
- Write down three ways in which it could be improved.
- What difference would these changes make to your mind and your body?

Sleep Well

Good quality sleep is essential. Many of us do not sleep well, particularly women who are expected to be ‘super’ in all aspects of their busy lives. Some people find it difficult to get off to sleep, others wake up during the night worrying about things, or wake up early in the morning and cannot get back to sleep.

To help us sleep better we can:

- Remove the television from the bedroom. If we fall asleep with the television on, the sound of the programmes, which are usually of a sexual or violent nature late at night, will penetrate our subconscious and disturb our peace of mind
- Prepare mentally for going to bed by relaxing for 30 minutes beforehand. We can have a bath, listen to soothing music, read something light, do some gentle stretching exercises, massage ourselves
- Review the day and finish on a high note by thinking of something positive that happened during the day
- Avoid caffeine and other stimulants in the evening and instead drink warm water or chamomile tea
- Keep paper and pen by our bedside. If we wake up in the night worried about something we have forgotten to do, we can write it down and then relax and go back to sleep.

PAUSE FOR THOUGHT

- Write down three things you could do to improve the quality of your sleep?
- Which one will you implement first?

Mental Sharpening

Later on in this book we will be looking at the impact of thoughts in some detail but there are some additional general points that can be made here.

Just like we need to be careful about the food we eat, we also need to be careful about our mental diet, that is the things that we read, watch or listen to. If we live off a diet of violent films, video games, pornography, mindless entertainment, gossip, the vitriol of some of the social media, or distressing stories in the daily news, then we are highly likely to become stressed, anxious and maybe depressed.

It is important to protect our mind from such harmful influences. How can we do this?

We can choose to:

- Limit the use of our mobile phones, laptops and other forms of entertainment
- Unsubscribe from some of our social media accounts
- Listen to, or read about, what's happening in the world just once a day rather than every hour like many of us do
- Read uplifting and inspiring books and articles
- Watch feel-good movies
- Listen to relaxing music

- Play games and have fun
- Laugh
- Dance
- Walk in nature
- Avoid, if we can, people who are always complaining and talking detrimentally about others
- Keep a journal in which we can express and download our fears and worries as well as our hopes and dreams.
- Spend time alone in silence giving our mind a much-needed break.
- Meditate
- Practice mindfulness.

PAUSE FOR THOUGHT

- Write down three actions you will take to protect your mind and boost your energy.

Social And Emotional Sharpening

It is important to have friends, relations, work colleagues, or other people whose company we enjoy. When we are depressed, we often feel lonely and cut off from others. In these circumstances, it is particularly important to open up to someone we can trust, who will listen and not judge us. If there is no one in our circle with whom we feel able to share, we can always contact the Samaritans, or some other mental health group or charity, or go online and checkout local meet-up groups.

Another way to break down the walls of isolation is do some kind of voluntary work. In giving we will receive and create a win/win situation for others and ourselves.

PAUSE FOR THOUGHT

- Write down the names of three people you can turn to for emotional support.
- What organisations or groups could you turn to for help?
- How do you, or could you, help other people?

Spiritual Sharpening

Stephen Covey highlights the important part spirituality can play in personal self-management. In particular, he urges us to be aware of our core human values (e.g. justice, creativity, freedom) that drive and motivate much of our behavior and give us a sense of purpose and mission. As already mentioned, when we don't know where we are going and what we want to achieve with our life, we feel dissatisfied, frustrated and unhappy. This book is all about how to rediscover and sharpen the spiritual aspect of the saw of our life.

Some of my key values are equality, fairness, justice and love. These values have led to a belief that all human beings should be treated with dignity and respect and encouraged to fulfill their potential, regardless of age, race, gender, sexual orientation, physical or mental ability.

Throughout my life I have always been on the side of the oppressed and done my best to make things better in whatever way I could, whether as a prison governor, social worker or as a citizen. As a result I have been, and still can be, very challenging, especially to people in authority!

With hindsight, I can see how my values have shaped my life. I have always wanted to help people and I have had no interest in earning lots of money, or being promoted. I have changed careers when no longer able to fulfill my values and, eventually, I became a stress management trainer in order to support my work as a volunteer with the Brahma Kumaris, which seeks to transform the whole world through the value of peace.

PAUSE FOR THOUGHT

- What really matters to you in this world?
- What are the main values underlying your answer?

- How do you feel when you act in accordance with your inner values?
- How do you feel when your values are suppressed, ignored or unfulfilled?

SUMMARY

There is an intimate connection between our mind and our body. The two are constantly communicating with each other. If we can tune in and listen to our body and our mind, we will be able to understand what is going on and take steps to restore peace to our mind and our body.

By sharpening the saw and renewing the four dimensions of our being, we will improve the quality of our mental health and general wellbeing.

STEP 2.
THINK POSITIVELY

Depression is a disease of thoughts.

Matt Haig

ALL HUMAN BEINGS have within them a very powerful resource, namely the ability to think and create thoughts. Thoughts are the foundation of our life. Everything we feel, say, or do begins with a thought.

Through our thoughts and associated feelings we create our life. As the well-known saying goes '*the quality of our thoughts determines the quality of our life*'.

We may not be able to control the events that happen in our life but we always have a choice as to how we see and handle them.

The events may be *external,* for example losing a job, a bereavement, a car crash, or *internal*, such as negative thoughts and feelings about our self or others.

Often our thought patterns are so deeply ingrained and feel so normal and natural that we think there is no other way. We become trapped in a prison of our own making. We feel hopeless and helpless, victims of a harsh and uncaring world in which there is no peace of mind.

Here are some suggestions to help you change your thinking and so change your mind and your life.

BECOME AWARE OF YOUR THOUGHTS

Thoughts are the seeds of depression or mental health. Like any other seeds the more attention we give them, the more they grow and eventually they bear fruit.

What sort of seeds are you sowing and growing in your mind?

In order to live a happy life, it is essential to be aware of what is going on in our mind and, in particular, to know the difference between positive and negative thoughts.

Positive thinking is about creating thoughts that make us feel happy and empowered. Thoughts like:

- Appreciating people and the beauty in this world
- Being grateful for all the good things we have in our life
- Accepting the things over which we have no control
- Focusing on solutions to the challenges we face
- Making the best of every situation and looking for the benefits in it
- Having an inspiring vision of ourselves and our future.

Such thoughts make us feel good, raise our energy levels and improve our health and relationships.

Negative thinking creates fear, tension and anxiety in our mind; it makes us ill and spoils our relationships. This is why it is so important to avoid any form of criticism, complaint, blame, comparison, gossip or judgment of others and ourselves.

Racism, sexism, nationalism, homophobia, or one religion thinking it is better than another are all forms of negative thinking. This poison in the mind is responsible for much of the despair and conflict in the world today.

The roots of many forms of depression, anxiety and stress are negative thoughts and feelings about ourselves and/or others.

Such thoughts infect our attitude, perceptions and beliefs and create a perfect storm in our mind that pollutes our way of seeing and being. We become like a fly trapped in a spider's web. The more we struggle, the worse it gets!

MORE ABOUT POSITIVE THOUGHTS

If positive thoughts are to be successful they must be:

- Focused on the here and now e.g. "I am kind" not "I will be kind".
- Unqualified e.g. "I am caring" not "I am sometimes caring".
- Beneficial to the self and others e.g. "I let go and move on"

- Without any negatives e.g. "I am always content", rather than "I am not unhappy".

Positive thinking also includes the use of:

Affirmations

Affirmations are life-affirming, positive statements about the self, which we repeat many times a day in order to replace negative patterns of thinking.

Rhyming ones are the best as the subconscious mind cannot reject them.

For example 'I am calm and free. And let things be'.

PAUSE FOR THOUGHT

- Create your own affirmation that you can carry around with you and use in times of need.

Visualisation

Without realising it, we often use the power of our imagination to pre-determine what is going to happen in our life. For example, we can keep imagining that one day we will be happy and healthy, or we can constantly visualise being sad and lonely for the rest of our life. Whichever we choose will become a self-fulfilling prophecy.

PAUSE FOR THOUGHT

- How do you visualise your future?
- How does it make you feel?
- If it's not so good, how could you change it for the better?
- If you had the time and unlimited resources to do what you wanted, what would you love to do?

DEVELOP A POSITIVE MENTAL ATTITUDE

Our attitude is like a preset programme in the mind - the default position that we automatically and consistently adopt to everything that is occurring in our life. This is best illustrated by the famous example of the glass, which contains water up to the half way level.

People with a positive mental attitude will see the glass as ‘half full’. Those with a negative attitude will see the glass as ‘half empty’. Who is right? The answer is both. However, the consequences of seeing it one way rather than the other are very different. Those who see the glass as ‘half full’ are more likely to share the contents with others, while those who see it as ‘half empty’ are less likely to do so because there’s not much left.

PAUSE FOR THOUGHT

- Are you a half full or half empty type of person?
- Are you an optimist or a pessimist?
- If the latter, what could you do to become more optimistic?

LOOK FOR THE BEST IN YOURSELF AND OTHERS

Closely related to *attitude* is *perception.* All of us have a 'good' side to our personality, like kindness, generosity and creativity, but there are also the 'bad' bits like anger, sadness and selfishness.

If we perceive ourselves to be 'worthless' or 'useless' to the exclusion of the better aspects of our personality, we are condemning ourselves to a life of misery because *where the attention goes energy flows.* If we shift our perception and attention away from the negative aspects of our self and focus more on the 'nicer' bits within us and others, we will experience a shift in the darkness of our mind and the quality of our life will automatically improve. By valuing and appreciating ourselves we will also naturally value and appreciate others and create a window of opportunity for acts of kindness and love.

PAUSE FOR THOUGHT

- Write down three negative words that you often use to describe yourself.
- Notice how you feel when you think of yourself in this way.
- Write down three words to describe the 'nicer' bits of you.
- How do you feel when you see yourself in this way?
- Which way do you prefer to see yourself? Why?

CHALLENGE UNHELPFUL BELIEFS

A belief is an opinion or conviction that we hold to be true. Beliefs help us navigate our way through life. They help us to make sense of things and guide our behavior. Many of our beliefs originate in childhood. As little children we were like sponges and automatically absorbed them from the people around us. As adults we rarely question their truth, or relevance to our own life. Like hand-me-down clothes, they may have outgrown their usefulness. Deeply rooted in our subconscious mind they often rule and ruin our life.

For example, if we have been brought up with the belief that 'I am stupid' or 'I am bad' (the black sheep of the family) our self esteem and self confidence are likely to be low and we will look out for and focus on only those situations which reinforce this belief. Consequently we will be prone to feelings of loneliness and alienation, which are the seedbed of depression.

PAUSE FOR THOUGHT

- Write down three negative core beliefs that you have about yourself and/or the world.
- What is the impact/effect of these beliefs on your life?
- Imagine how you would feel if you no longer had these beliefs.

CHANGE EXPECTATIONS INTO HOPE

Unfulfilled expectations or desires are a major cause of much unhappiness, whether in the form of depression, stress or anxiety.

Expectations are often a way of trying to control other people or situations. The more insecure and uncertain we feel, the more importance we are likely to attach to the fulfillment of our expectations. They help us feel secure. When people fail to respond in a way that we consider to be appropriate, or things do not work out as we want, we react with disappointment, hurt, frustration and anger. A-type personalities (for whom everything is either black or white and has to be done now) and perfectionists find it particularly challenging when things do not go their way.

Other people, of course, also have expectations of us and the failure to live up to each other's expectations leads to much unhappiness and anger and plays a major role in divorce and suicide rates as well as strained relationships between people, communities and countries.

We all have countless expecations about everything and anything. Often we are not even aware of them until something happens to expose them and upset our peace of mind; whether it's the train being late, extreme weather conditions, shortages of basic commodities, or family and friends taking us for granted.

One solution to the challenge of expectations is not to have any! They are often more trouble than they are worth. If we wish, we can replace expectations with hope and acceptance. Once we realise that *we cannot control anything or anyone except our self,* hope and acceptance become attractive alternatives.

Hope is more positive, fluid and flexible than expectations. It enables us to be less attached to outcomes.

For example, if *I expect* to meet my friend in the park for a walk in the morning and she cancels at the last minute, I am likely to feel let down, hurt or rejected and I could be upset for the rest of the day - blaming or criticising her for being so selfish, or thoughtless, or whatever.

If, on the other hand, I *hope* to meet my friend and things do not work out as planned, I will be more able to accept the situation, rearrange the time and date of our next meeting and then make alternative plans for the day. This might involve visiting an art gallery by myself or contacting other friends to see if anyone is free to come for a walk or meet up for a coffee. In this scenario there is no blame, judgement or build-up of resentment to spoil our relationship.

Accepting the things we cannot change as well as changing the things we can, is a very powerful way of staying calm and reducung our anxiety and stress. We cannot make people like us or do what we want. Instead of banging our head against a brick wall and making our life a misery, we can find other ways to influence situations and create better outcomes for ourself and others. A flexible, humble, patient, assertive and considerate approach based on mutual respect and understanding can work wonders.

Having said all this, it is important to have clear standards of behaviour in order to manage different areas of life but these need to be agreed and applied in a logical and reasonable way with, ideally, the consent of all those involved.

Likewise, it is important not to beat ourselves up when we fail to meet our own exacting standards. Acceptance, encouragement, compassion and a gentle push towards the goals we seek to achieve are far better than self-flagellation or depression!

PAUSE FOR THOUGHT

- Write down three expectations that you have of yourself or others.
- How do you feel when these expectations are not met?
- How do you behave?
- In what ways could you change your expectations so that you remain stable and happy regardless of what happens in your life?

REMEMBER — YOU HAVE A CHOICE

Whether we realise it or not, we always have a choice as to how we deal with any situation. Knowing this is very liberating. It offers us hope.

The choice is ultimately between what can be called the GLAD way (giving, loving, accepting, detached) or the SAD way (stressed, angry/anxious or depressed). The implications of this are very deep.

PAUSE FOR THOUGHT

- In the light of what you have read so far, can anyone or anything 'make' you depressed, anxious or stressed?

If we are aware of alternative ways of thinking and being and are able to *respond* rather than *react* to the triggers that disturb our peace of mind, then, at least in theory, nothing or no one can make us depressed, anxious or stressed because there are always other options open to us.

For example, we can choose to:

- Acknowledge and accept our feelings rather than suppress them
- Release our feelings by talking about them to someone we trust
- Learn to assert ourselves and claim our right to be treated with dignity and respect

- Look at things in a more detached way
- Understand the bigger picture
- See things from other people's point of view
- Accept the things that can't be changed
- Stop beating ourselves up
- Put an end to the vicious cycle of negative thinking
- Stop catastrophising
- Forgive those who have hurt us
- Be kind to ourselves and practice self compassion
- Meditate
- Practice mindfulness.

Of course, these things are easier said than done. It does require courage, determination and inner power to overcome negative ways of thinking and being.

PAUSE FOR THOUGHT

- What are the underlying thoughts and feelings that cause you to feel stressed, anxious or depressed?
- What action could you take to shift your mind-set and improve the quality of your life?

For me, reclaiming my power by ending the blame game and letting go of seeing myself as a victim of life, has been crucial in dealing with depression.

During the time I was a social worker, I was off work for six months due to stress and depression. At the time I was mentally, physically and emotionally exhausted. Initially I blamed my manager for giving me a very challenging caseload.

When I spent time reflecting on my situation, I realised that the reason why I had such a high caseload was because I was afraid to say ‘No’ for fear of being punished or rejected in some way. I then realised that I could not say ‘No’ to anyone else either! I was constantly running around trying to pacify and please everyone.

Thinking about the reasons for this, I discovered that I was desperate for approval. I had no self-respect or self-confidence due to a deep feeling of being unworthy and unlovable. Keeping people happy was a way of avoiding the risk of being reminded of my fundamental insecurity.

Counselling, positive thinking, assertiveness training and meditation were the tools I used to change my mind-set and learn to accept and appreciate my self without the need for approval from others. I was able to step into my own power and recognise my right to express my feelings and thoughts and put down boundaries and say 'No' when necessary, without feeling guilty or inadequate. I cannot claim that it was easy and it certainly did not happen overnight, but change did come and the depression has gone.

SUMMARY

The way we think about things has a huge impact on our mental health, either lifting or crushing our spirits, depending on the type of thoughts we create in our mind.

If we wish to escape the mental hell of negative perceptions, beliefs and attitudes and replace them with positive ones, it is essential that we take a step back and look at our thoughts, check them and, if they are doing us harm, change them. This process is known as *Check and Change.*

It does take time and effort to change the thinking of a lifetime but the rewards are worth it.

The more powerful, positive and uplifting we make our thoughts and actions, the happier we will be. Our energy will rise and with a can do attitude we will feel inspired to break through the darkness that is holding us back.

STEP 3. BECOME SOUL CONSCIOUS

Your vision will become clear only when you can look into your own heart. Who looks outside, dreams: who looks inside, awakes.

Carl Jung

SOUL CONSCIOUSNESS is about being aware of our self as an eternal spiritual being. It is the key to ending the darkness that grips the mind and heart.

In this hedonistic, busy world there are so many pressures, choices, distractions and complications that it is easy to lose sight of the deeper meaning and purpose of our existence. We can end up just drifting or sleep-walking our way through life. The years flash by and, before we know it, we are in old age wondering where the time went; perhaps full of regrets for not doing or being our best and wondering what happens next? Extinction? Or Immortality?

If we see ourselves as just another species on this earth that comes and goes like a briefly flickering candle, life can feel quite scary, meaningless and, ultimately, quite depressing. In these circumstances, it is not surprising that we try to hold on to our youth and good looks and do whatever it takes to feel happy and secure. We often relieve our anxieties through different forms of consumerism - new clothes, a lovely home, a car, holidays abroad, lots of good food and drink, not to mention the delights of music, films, video games and other forms of entertainment.

If we appreciate ourselves for *who we are* rather than *what we look like,* or *what we do*; if we value our strengths and inner qualities and feel good about ourselves and our life, we will radiate a natural beauty through our eyes and sense of wellbeing that transcends the need for external fixes.

Here are some ways to develop greater self-awareness and move to a higher consciousness where we accept ourselves and see our depressive feelings in a new light.

REMEMBER WHO YOU REALLY ARE

One of the most important questions we can ever ask ourselves is,

'Who am I?'

Do you know who you are?

PAUSE FOR THOUGHT

Imagine you are creating a Facebook page or writing to someone you have met on the Internet. Write down a list of 16 things to describe yourself.

Now cross off any points relating to your

- Body (age, gender, sexuality, race, nationality, appearance, physical and mental condition etc.),
- Roles in life (job, relationships etc.),
- Possessions (house, car, pets etc.),
- Hobbies and interests
- Belief systems (political, religious etc.)
- Any negative points about your personality (grumpy, tired, etc.).

Do you have anything left on your list?

Hopefully, there will be some positive qualities such as kind, generous, caring, etc. These qualities form part of your original good self. They are part of your spiritual DNA.

If you were unable to come up with 16 points, it indicates that you do not know yourself very well. In other words, you are living with a stranger!

What do all the points you crossed off have in common? They all relate to your external world and they are, therefore, all transient and subject to change.

Spirituality is about exploring our inner world, recognising and giving attention to our pure essence. As is often said, *we are spiritual beings having a human experience, rather than human beings having a spiritual experience.*

Many of us have lost awareness of and connection to our higher self. This can cause us to feel sad, lonely and depressed. We then identify with the depression and say 'I am depressed'.

From a spiritual perspective, it is more accurate to say *'I am a soul who feels depressed'.*

This understanding creates a space in our mind, which allows us to dis-identify from the depression and deal with it in a more manageable way. Depression is only a part of who I am.

Detaching in a loving way, or being a silent witness, to whatever is going on in our mind and our life, is a very powerful tool for healing ourselves and reducing our pain and suffering - physical, mental and emotional.

I used to get very upset and angry about all sorts of things to do with myself and/or other people. Whether it was illness, lack of money, people letting me down, or the way other people were treating each other, I would quickly go down the road of complaining, criticising, or judging. Someone or something was always to blame and it was all so unfair.

Nowadays, I do my best to practice being non-judgemental, seeing events as neither good nor bad. I love the phrase 'It is what it is'. Whether I am ill or unhappy, or other people are angry with me, or each other, everything is okay. There is no point in resenting or resisting what is.

Removing the subjectivity and, at the same time, having good wishes for others and ourselves, enables us to find ways to make things better without disturbing our peace of mind. It also saves a lot of time and energy (mental and emotional).

EXPERIMENT

- Sit comfortably
- Breathe slowly, deeply and gently
- On the screen of your mind see yourself looking at yourself as a curious observer/friend

- Describe what you see and feel in the third person...(your name) is looking...
- S/he is feeling...
- S/he wants to...
- Empathise with...(your name)
- Say something encouraging to...(your name)
- Give yourself a hug
- Notice how you now feel about yourself.

FEED YOUR SOUL

The soul needs nurturing, just like the physical body does. It thrives on awareness, focused attention, silence, stillness and inner peace.

Many of our habits and behaviours are driven by *unmet spiritual needs* such as the need for lasting security, peace, happiness or love.

Often we seek to satisfy these 'soul needs' through attachment to other people and the pleasurable effects of good company, food, alcohol, drugs, shopping, music, sport and other activities.

However, *spiritual needs cannot be satisfied in the long-term through material means.* Sooner or later, we will experience a feeling that something is lacking, that things are not as good as they could be.

Deep inside on a subconscious level, we know that we have been much happier and more peaceful and loving than we are now.

Eventually the pain and longing for something better becomes so intense that we feel compelled to begin a different search along 'the road less travelled' into ourselves.

Like a rat in a maze, whether we like it or not, the drama of our life pushes us out of blind alleyways and in the direction of soul consciousness.

We begin to ask ourselves important questions:

Why is my life such a mess?

How can I overcome these feelings of …?

When and how will it all end?

What is life really all about?

When we take time out to consider such questions through reflection, contemplation, meditation or prayer, we start to become calmer, more peaceful and aware. Answers and insights will come into our mind because everything is inside us waiting to be discovered and revealed.

If we give ourselves the time and space to listen, our quiet inner voice will guide and protect us.

Whenever I have to make an important decision about anything and I am confused, I always take time out to sit quietly and ask myself and the One what I should do.

Sometimes I get an intuitive feeling straight away as to what needs to be done. On other occasions, the answer emerges over time through conversations with others, or my attention being drawn to a book, article or something which signals the way ahead. Rather than rushing into something, which I might later regret, I do my best to go with the flow of my feelings. If something does not feel comfortable, or I have any doubts, I do not do it. If I get a surge of energy or enthusiasm, then I will do it. In this way I feel guided and supported and life becomes an exciting adventure.

For example, some years ago, I occasionally thought of moving from my first floor flat on a housing estate. One day, passing an estate agent's window, I happened to notice a picture of a ground floor sitting room overlooking a beautiful garden. The flat was being offered for sale at a much lower price than the market value of my own flat. Out of curiosity I went into the estate agent, had an immediate viewing and put an offer on the flat, which was accepted. Within two hours my life had been turned upside down! And just over a year later, I moved into what is a much nicer, quieter place in a better and more convenient location.

When we awaken in this way, life has greater meaning and depth. Our consciousness expands and we are more able to break out of the black hole of self-pity, anger, loathing and shame that often lies at the heart of depression. We become aware that stress, anxiety, unhappiness or depression is not who we are. *It is an experience we are going through. Sooner or later it will end.*

We see things in a new and more connected way.

I am a soul and I occupy a body[10].

---

[10]The subtitle of Bill Bryson's book 'The Body' is 'A Guide For Occupants', which immediately raises the question as to who, or what, is occupying the body.

Every human being is also a soul and we are all connected, part of one great global spiritual family.

More and more, we begin to see that everything has spiritual significance. The shell of our ego breaks and we open ourselves up to new understandings and ways of thinking. Such as:

- The law of karma (we reap what we sow)
- The nature of the Divine
- The importance of forgiveness and compassion and other spiritual practices in healing ourselves and the world
- Seeing life as a drama or a play designed to bring out the best in each of us
- The power of spiritual energy in creating and sustaining the world
- The inter-connection of everything on the planet and beyond.

In Hinduism this process of spiritual awakening is known as 'opening the third eye'. We have two physical eyes for seeing this physical world and a spiritual eye for 'seeing' things beyond the sense organs. Symbolically this is represented in the form of a small round tilak, or dot, which some Hindus wear in the centre of their forehead as a reminder to be aware of the self, and each human being, as a soul i.e. to be soul conscious.

Seeing ourselves as a tiny dot of shining light, like a diamond or star, in the centre of the forehead and behind the eyes is a useful meditation technique.

Meditation is the best way to recharge and nurture the soul.

EXPERIMENT

- Sit comfortably in a quiet, welcoming space
- Take several deep, slow breaths to relax your body
- Turn your attention inwards
- Imagine that there is a tiny point of light shining in the centre of your forehead
- Draw all the energy in your body up to this point
- Focus on the point
- Allow yourself to become still
- Say slowly to yourself several times...I...am...a...peaceful... soul
- Feel the peace
- Enjoy the peace
- Be peace
- Slowly bring your attention back into the room
- Notice how different you feel.

UNDERSTAND WHAT'S REALLY GOING ON

Seeing life through our 'third eye' turns challenges into opportunities to develop our spiritual 'muscles' - such as faith, courage, determination, love, resilience, forgiveness, patience and tolerance. We begin to see the benefit in everything. There are lessons to be learned, debts to be repaid, relationships to be healed and many chances to practice self-love, appreciation and acceptance.

Our worst enemy becomes our best friend as they reveal all the resentment, anger, intolerance and ego that needs clearing inside if we are to reclaim our peace of mind.

The pain of depression, anxiety or stress becomes a gift to be unwrapped, a messenger to tell us we have gone off track and a reminder to go within and return to our original state of peace and love.

If we did not have such challenges how could we become wise and strong inside?

PAUSE FOR THOUGHT

- What is the message behind the feelings you are currently experiencing?
- What lessons have you learned about yourself and others through being anxious, stressed or depressed?

PRACTICE YOUR VIRTUES

The word 'virtue' in this day and age sounds rather dated, something from a bygone era when more people used to go to church and had the aim of being and doing good in their life.

Virtues are part of our original goodness and an expression of different aspects of the soul in action. Virtues are always positive. They have a life-enhancing impact on both the person who is being virtuous and the recipient.

David Hamilton in his book 'The Five Effects Of Kindness' demonstrates with scientific evidence the beneficial effect kindness has on the self and others. Not only does being kind release endorphins, which calm the body and make us feel good but the recipient too feels good and is inspired to act similarly. Such is the effect of a kind act that even someone witnessing one is uplifted and wants to follow suit!

According to The Virtues Project[11] there are one hundred virtues that we can access and practice. They include:

- Acceptance
- Accountability
- Compassion
- Contentment
- Courage
- Courtesy

[11]For further information about The Virtues Project see www.virtuesproject.com

- Creativity
- Detachment
- Determination
- Dignity
- Empathy
- Endurance
- Fairness
- Faith
- Flexibility
- Forgiveness
- Generosity
- Hope
- Humanity
- Humility
- Integrity
- Justice
- Joyfulness
- Kindness
- Love
- Loyalty
- Mercy
- Optimism
- Patience
- Resilience
- Respect
- Responsibility
- Self-discipline
- Serenity
- Thoughtfulness
- Understanding
- Wonder

Feeling depressed, anxious or stressed presents us with many opportunities to use these different virtues. We just need to be aware of them and then, of course, put them into practice.

It might feel strange at first, especially if we are not used to thinking outside the box in this way.

Who is the first and most important person we have to practice our virtues on? Our self. Many of us have treated ourselves badly for years. We have been our own worst enemy rather than our own best friend. We have given too much power to the inner critic and consequently have been blind to the better aspects of our self.

Now is the time to be kind, sweet, gentle, caring, encouraging, loving, appreciative and accepting of ourselves and those who seek to help us.

PAUSE FOR THOUGHT

- Think of someone you really admire; they can be living or dead, famous or not
- Write-down three of their qualities or virtues that you really like
- Imagine what it would be like if you were like them
- Notice how you feel.

Hopefully, you have enjoyed doing this exercise and it made you feel good. Why was this? Because you were really thinking about yourself! The qualities we are attracted to in others are a reflection of our own! We can only admire or identify with something if it resonates with some aspect of our self. As the saying goes 'If you spot it, you've got it'.

When I was first introduced to this exercise, I refused to accept the answers. My self-esteem was so low that I could not believe that I had the qualities of my hero, Gandhi, in my own nature. I loved his non-violent approach to life, his leadership skills, ability to analyse things and create radical, practical solutions, his courage, authenticity and determination to overcome injustice. However, on reflection, stepping back and reviewing the content of my life, I could see traces of courage, faith in the goodness of people and determination to overcome injustice in creative, peaceful ways.

REMEMBER THE MANTRA 'OM SHANTI'

A mantra is a sacred word or phrase, which has special power and enables its user to connect with their inner world. Mantras are often associated with Hinduism , or Eastern-based meditation practices such as transcendental meditation.

One of the most powerful mantras is 'Om Shanti'.

'Om' is a Sanskrit word for 'soul' and is considered to be the first and most sacred sound of creation - its vibrational frequency is revered.

The word 'shanti' is Hindi for 'peace', a state of being in which there is no conflict or desire, distaste or dislike - just stillness, contentment and complete acceptance of everything as it is.

'Om' and 'Shanti' complement each other perfectly and when combined remind us of the true nature of the soul.

Om shanti. I am a peaceful soul.

When practiced as a mantra it can take us beyond this physical/material world into a space where we remain aware but detached, seeing things clearly with an unlimited spiritual perspective.

When the going gets tough, 'Om Shanti' can be used like a switch to refocus ourselves and remind us of how we are meant to be. It is the perfect antidote to depression, stress or anxiety.

EXPERIMENT

- Sit quietly
- Breathe slowly, deeply and gently
- Imagine someone gently and lovingly whispering the mantra 'Om Shanti' in your ear
- Keep repeating the mantra with feeling
- Allow the mantra to quieten your mind and fill your heart with peace
- Bring your attention back into the room
- Notice the difference in your feelings.

PAUSE FOR THOUGHT

- Think of a situation in your life where the mantra 'Om Shanti' could make a real difference to the way you see and handle things.
- How would it help?

SUMMARY

Opening the third eye can be life-saving and life-changing for someone who is experiencing depression, anxiety or stress. It helps us to understand some of the roots of our darkness and offers empowering and enlightening ways to shift into a happier way of living and being.

We can become calm and content again by:

- Recognising and remembering our spiritual nature
- Making time to nurture our soul
- Seeing our distress as an opportunity to go within and explore its hidden gifts
- Practicing being virtuous with ourselves and others
- Taking support from the mantra 'Om shanti'

In these ways opening 'the third eye' can be the start of a new adventure in living. Like anything else that is worth doing, it does require some effort and commitment. It is very easy to fall asleep again!

STEP 4.
CONNECT WITH THE LIGHT

"Truth sees God, and wisdom contemplates God,
and from these two comes a third,
a holy and wonderful delight in God, who is love."

Julian of Norwich, *Revelations of Divine Love*

AWAKENING TO OUR HIGHER CONSCIOUSNESS, opens up the possibility of exploring *supra consciousness* i.e. awareness of and relationship with the ultimate Source of peace, love and joy. This Being is often referred to as God, the Light, the Divine, the Universal Mind, the Big Intelligence, the One, Allah, Shiva, the Supreme Soul, or Supreme Being.

For most of the history of humanity, the idea of connecting with such a Being was taken for granted. People of different faiths came together for worship and celebration and put their behaviour in a wider context, emphasising the importance of living together in peace and love in accordance with the teachings of their Founder. People who were distressed or unhappy in any way could seek spiritual guidance, or pray to their god for help.

We are now living in very different times. Despite the exhortation of the different faith traditions, the world is becoming a more restless and peaceless place.

With the rise of the power of science many question the existence of God. Others find it difficult to engage with a Being in whose name many wars have been have been fought and countless atrocities committed.

In some religions there may now be less emphasis on a wrathful, vengeful God but the legacy lives on in the psyche of many and is reinforced by the guilt and shame of being a 'sinner'.

Consequently, in the West, many people have walked away and sought solace elsewhere; in therapy, counselling, personal growth and development and the alternatives offered by the mind, body and spirit industry and eco spirituality. Despite these welcome developments, at the end of the day we are left to our own devices and may still feel confused, alone and prone to anxiety and depression with no answers to the ultimate questions of life and death.

In my search for peace and happiness, I have explored Buddhism with its emphasis on peace through detachment and compassion and also Hinduism. I love visiting India where there is not one God but many. People delight in worshipping a variety of gods and, in particular, goddesses some of whom are symbolically depicted riding on a lion, sitting on a swan, or floating on a lotus leaf! India may have its challenges of poverty and oppression but the people know in their hearts that they are loved by their gods, whom they believe shower them with everything they need to get by in this life and beyond. Consequently they respond with a deep natural love, or bhavna, for their deities, which is expressed in vibrant dance, music, art and a huge variety of temples and countless roadside shrines. Their flexible approach to God and religion has enabled them to survive two periods of colonisation (by Muslims and Christians). It is also interesting to note that India, so far, has never invaded another country.

What's all this got to do with breaking through the darkness of depression, anxiety or stress?

If we can find or make a connection with the One who gives unconditional love, the power to change ourselves and takes us beyond this physical world and the pain and loneliness of depression, then surely it is very relevant?

How can we do this?

Here are some ways for you to consider and experiment with:

OPEN YOUR MIND

Being aware of our self as a soul is an important precondition to connecting with the Light but in itself it is not sufficient.

If we wish to explore the possibility of there being a God to whom we can connect, then it is very important to have an open mind. If we have very fixed and rigid ideas and beliefs about the non-existence of God then making any kind of link to the Divine will not be possible.

As we have seen, our beliefs are the filter through which we experience life. If we believe that there is no such thing as a God, we will close the door to any possible relationship unless, or until, we have a profound experience that shatters and changes our belief. For example, the conversion of St Paul on the road to Damascus.

If we are agnostic or have an open mind about God, then we can consider the many ideas of who or what God is. Some think He is omnipresent i.e. everywhere - even in the pebbles and stones! Some think that we are all part of one cosmic being. In India women were, until recently, expected to treat their husband as their god and guru. For the Muslims, God is imageless and for the Buddhists and the sannyasis of India there is no God but rather a stream of consciousness into which we will one day merge when we have achieved perfection. Christians believe in God but His form is a mystery.

Despite these differences, there is general consensus that God is a being of love and light. He is the Lord and Master of all creation and we are His children. As such we must honour and obey Him or else! Believers express their devotion through praying, chanting and singing as well as bowing and kneeling and other gestures of respect, humility and love. Without doubt, such practices bring a lot of comfort and relief to many.

Rightly or wrongly, this approach does not appeal to everyone.

We are living in exciting times when many of us are free to explore and consider who or what God means to us without fear of being burnt at the stake, imprisoned or condemned to hell forever. We are free to go on our own journey of discovery through reading, prayer, contemplation, meditation, retreats, pilgrimages and communing with nature. Sooner or later, we will reach our destination and know the truth about God.

My own understanding and belief is that God is a soul just like all of us. As such He/She does not have a gender or any of the other things we ticked off in the 'Who Am I?' exercise.

That Soul is supreme in that it never takes a body and so never loses its power. Staying beyond the drama of this world in which we all get involved and trapped, the Supreme Soul is able to support, guide and love us. The communication is through pure thoughts and powerful vibrations. When we are 'soul conscious' we can tune into and receive this energy. Effective communication also requires an honest heart and a true desire to know and love the One who only wants the best for us.

Just like we phone our friends and family on our mobile phone at anytime or anywhere, we can also communicate with the One. We transmit and receive vibrations through the power of a silent mind.

PAUSE FOR THOUGHT

- What are your thoughts and feelings about God?
- Reflect on your own life and write down any special/ unusual spiritual experiences you have had.
- What happened?
- How did you feel?
- What impact has the experience had on your life?

If you have not had any special spiritual experiences, or you have doubts about the whole God thing then, for a moment, imagine what your life would be like if such a Being did exist.

Alternatively, sit in silence, connect with your higher self and reach out to the Divine and see what happens.

ALIGN WITH THE DIVINE

As we have seen in Step 3, each of us is a unique soul with our own needs and beliefs. In everyone's life there comes a time, sooner or later, when we hit a brick wall and feel we can't go on in the same old ways. Something has to change. We need some extra powerful help and support. Being depressed, very anxious, or stressed is one of those times.

Would you like to be understood, accepted, valued, appreciated, supported, empowered and encouraged by Someone who focuses on your strengths, rather than your weaknesses? Someone who has a pure vision as to who and what you are?

Would you like to have a relationship with Someone who never lets you down and is hugely patient, accepting and forgiving, even when you kick and scream and blame them for all that you have suffered in this life?

Is it really possible to have such a relationship?

Throughout history there are examples of people, who have experienced the beauty and bliss of the Divine, either within or outside organised religion. For example Julian of Norwich, Rumi, Khalil Gibran.

In our own time, numerous people have had out of body, or near death experiences, and have been overwhelmed by the love of the Light, which has transformed their life forever[12].

---

[12]For example see Dying to Be Me by Anita Moorjani.

Anyone can have a deep connection with the Divine if they truly want one. As the old sayings go 'Seek and you will find' and 'When the student is ready the teacher appears'.

For example, a connection with the God of your understanding is a key element in the success of Alcoholics Anonymous and similar groups. Members acknowledge and accept their addiction and surrender themselves to a Higher Power and in return receive the courage, determination and strength to stop their addiction and change their life.

In my own case, I had explored and exhausted most avenues before I came across Raja Yoga meditation as taught by the Brahma Kumaris.

The teachings are very simple but deep:

Consider yourself to be a soul and then in this awareness remember the Supreme Soul, the One who is an infinite point source of pure love, peace and joy.

Every Brahma Kumaris centre has a meditation space with a picture of the Supreme Soul represented as a point of radiant golden light against a red background.

When I was first introduced to the Divine in this way, all I could say was "I hate you" because of all the things that had been done to me in God's name when I was a child. Much to my amazement the image came alive and circles of pulsating light came towards me. I became very still and peaceful, filled with a very subtle healing energy. Then I knew for sure that there was something in this God business. Having had a taste of how I could be, I started to meditate and connect on a regular basis.

Being soul conscious is the key to aligning with the Divine as it enables us to tune in to the higher energy/vibrations of the Supreme Soul who exists in a dimension beyond the time and space of this limited world of matter. We go into the unlimited and our consciousness expands accordingly. Going beyond in this way gives us a totally different perspective on our self and our life. It brings clarity and detachment and a sense of freedom and hope.

EXPERIMENT

- Sit quietly by yourself
- Focus your eyes on a point on the wall or ceiling
- Breathe slowly, deeply and gently
- Create a peaceful space in your mind

- Disconnect your mind from every day life
- Remind yourself "I am a soul separate from but connected to this body"
- Visualise yourself as a tiny shining point of light in the centre of your forehead
- Imagine a golden ray of light connecting you, the soul, to the Light
- Open yourself to the Light
- Bathe in the Light
- Relax and fill yourself with peace, love and power
- When ready, slowly bring your attention back into the body
- Become aware of your surroundings
- Smile
- Notice any changes in your mind and body.

It takes awhile to master an exercise like this, so please be patient with yourself and keep practicing it a few times every day and you will begin to feel lighter and brighter.

REMEMBER TO SURRENDER

As has already been mentioned, at the heart of at least some forms of depression there is a lot of anger – anger against others and ourselves. Much of it comes from the pain of childhood experiences when we may have been abused, humiliated, ignored, bullied or rejected. Such experiences can cripple us for life. They shaped and moulded our psyche at a time when we were unable to defend ourselves, or understand what was really going on. Often we internalise the guilt and shame and blame ourselves for what has happened.

It's all my fault.

I deserved it.

I am such a bad person.

If only I had...

Inside most of us there is a little hurt child waiting to be heard and released from the pain of the past. Some of us deal with the pain through counselling or some sort of therapy. However, it does not always work and, in some cases, it may just reinforce the injustice of it all and lead to even greater anger, resentment and self-loathing.

Other people don't go there in the first place. It is just too painful to handle and they do their best to block it or push it into the depths of their subconscious, hoping that the memories and pain will go away. Of course, they don't and they won't until they are brought out of the cupboard and into the cold light of day.

So what can we do and how can the Light help?

In my experience, God is the greatest therapist. He does not judge or condemn us. He listens with love and respect. He takes away the tension, fear, rage, upset and regret, leaving us with a sense of release and peace. And it's all for free!! However, such help does come at a price.

God helps those who help themselves. In order for it to work we need to let go of the past i.e. the thoughts and feelings that are causing us pain and give it to Him. This is not an easy task to do. You can only let go of something if you know what you are holding on to and you want to let go of it.

Sometimes we don't want to let go of the past because we have so much invested in it - we can't imagine life without our painful story, our grudges and resentment and the victim badge that brings us so much attention and sympathy.

If we wish to let go of the past we need to revisit it, become aware of the pain and really acknowledge and accept it. This is best done during meditation when we are in the awareness of being a loving and detached soul in the presence of the Divine.

In this safe space we are able to ask for divine help to let go of the feelings attached to the negative events that have happened in our life. Once the feelings have been released, they no longer have any power over us. And we are more able to face, understand and learn from the events themselves and change our life.

Surrender in this way can take different forms. For example, we can:

- Talk to the God of our understanding and pour out all our feelings about whatever it is we want to release
- Use the power of our imagination to create a picture in our mind where, for example, we put all the angry feelings we are aware of in a box. This box keeps expanding until there is nothing left to put in it. We then seal the box and push it into a massive fire. As the contents of the box burn and turn to ash, we feel light, happy and free
- Write a letter to the Divine expressing all the regret and pain experienced in the story of our life. Then tear it up with love and bin it, or burn it.
- Pray for help, support, forgiveness, peace of mind, or whatever we feel we need at this moment in time
- Ask for the courage, determination and power to face and overcome our inner turmoil and become whole again.

I have done such exercises many times with participants in workshops and also by myself. They are very powerful and effective if we are honest and have a genuine desire to let go of things. Such exercises may have to be done numerous times because there is a lot to clear from our mind and our heart. Like an archeologist excavating an ancient site, we keep discovering new layers of rubbish that need to be removed in our search for the real treasure of lasting happiness, peace and love. We keep going because it makes us feel better and because we know that everything is coming up to say 'goodbye'. This latter point is very important.

Always remember we are bringing up the past not to reinforce it but to release it so it no longer has a hold over us.

EXPERIMENT

- Choose one of the above ways of surrendering the past
- Follow the suggested instructions
- Notice how good you feel afterwards.

RECHARGE YOURSELF

Every soul is on a journey of self-discovery and healing. The depth of our sorrow and unhappiness is a barometer of how loving and happy we have been at some stage in our life on this earth. The greater the sorrow, the greater the past happiness!

I believe in rebirth/reincarnation and I have come to the conclusion that people experiencing depression are probably older souls who have had more than one birth.

In this context, depression can be seen as the accumulative effect of a variety of experiences over several lifetimes during which the energy of the soul has become depleted and less able to deal with challenges in a positive and proactive way. Buried deep in our subconscious they have a subtle impact on the way we think and feel in the here and now.

The memories of past births can be accessed for those who choose through past life regression/therapy. This is not something I have done or would personally recommend. However, I have read about it and it does help some people to understand what's going on and why.

Another way to understand depression is through the law of entropy, namely everything goes from new to old and from order to chaos. In this context, the soul is like a battery whose energy has drained away, dissipated over time through the ups and downs of life. Just like our phones and laptops need recharging so does each soul - eventually. The older the soul, the greater the need for a recharge!

How do we do this?

The energy of the soul is expressed through vibrations. As we saw in Step 2, there is an intimate connection between our vibrations and our thoughts and feelings. Negative thoughts and feelings have adamaging effect on our mental and physical wellbeing and our relationships with others.

Putting a full stop to wasteful and negative thoughts and feelings will prevent the soul from losing more energy and will assist the process of recovery. However, this is not sufficient in itself to restore us to our former glory. We need to connect with a source of spiritual power greater than ourselves, a source of unlimited pure energy.

Just as we are learning to harness the power of the sun to generate pure energy and replace the harmful use of fossil fuels, we can learn to harness the power of the Divine to renew our spiritual energy without resorting to all the artificial stimulants and distractions commonly used to make ourselves feel better.

The purer our thoughts and feelings, the higher will be the quality of our vibrations.

In meditation, through awareness of our true spiritual identity, combined with focus and concentration, we can forge a link with the divine spiritual Sun. This enables us to receive powerful vibrations of love and peace, which will gradually replenish and heal the soul. The mechanism for this is God's grace.

The spiritual teacher and author, Anthony Strano, in his book 'The Man Who Loved Angels', best describes how grace works. This is what he has to say:

Grace is the magic ingredient that transforms everything. Grace is God's power. It is non-human. Although received through human thought it moves the mind and heart towards higher wisdom and love.

Grace can only come from God because only His being is unconditional. I need God's grace to transform. It is not enough just to make my own effort although that responsibility must be there.

Grace comes from the soul's vertical link to God, from conquering the intense gravity of a horizontal 'give and take' existence. Grace is God's direct co-operation.

Grace is a selfless, unconditional current of power that strengthens:

> *The mind, making it serene*
>
> *The will, making it determined*
>
> *The intellect, making it humble*
>
> *The feelings, making them clean.*

Grace is a gift given to the one who is honest with the self.

It is the spiritual alchemy that:

Dissolves the dirt in the mind and heart

Transforms mistakes into lessons

Creates the power to forgive the self

Makes the past truly past

Prevents remorse spoiling the best of today.

Grace frees the Self from the self. It recreates and replenishes the soul. It can uplift, re-generate and cleanse because it comes directly from God's Heart to my heart, from God's Mind to my mind.

Now is the time for the direct flow of God's transformative love.

Grace is the key ingredient for metamorphosis. It opens the door to unlimited possibilities. Miracles become the norm.

If I am careless, lazy or, especially, selfish, I cannot absorb God's grace when it is given. It is deflected.

I make no apologies for quoting this in full because Anthony Strano had a deep understanding of and loving relationship with the Divine and was able to express his experience in a clear, simple and moving way.

If we can open our mind and heart to God, we too will receive the power to recharge and reboot our soul and overcome the negative forces that have ruled us for so long and made us depressed.

EXPERIMENT

- Sit in silence
- Breathe slowly deeply and gently
- Become still, peaceful and serene
- See yourself as a tiny point of subtle energy
- Connect your mind and heart to the benevolent Light
- Bathe in its gentle glow
- Allow God's vibrations to work their magic
- After a minute bring your attention back into the room
- Notice how different you feel.

SHINE YOUR LIGHT

We were born happy, peaceful and loving. As we have seen, time has taken its toll and we have lost a lot of our sparkle.

The pain of feeling the contrast between how we were and how we are now can be a major cause of depression.

However, it is also a gift that can put us on the 'long and winding road' back to health and wholeness.

It is also a powerful incentive to keep going, despite the obstacles, because we know that what we were, we can become again.

We can go back to a future based on the truth of who we really are.

So far in this book we have explored ways of shifting the darkness by changing our thinking, being aware of our true spiritual nature and connecting with the Divine, the one who removes our burdens and recharges the battery of the soul back to its original condition.

Through this process we can become authentic. We will no longer need to *try* to be happy, peaceful and loving.

When our thoughts, feelings and actions move into alignment, we just *are* - like spiritual flowers or the sun, spreading unlimited peace and happiness wherever we go, regardless of the circumstances, or situations we find ourselves in.

Meditation plays an important part in this process. Through awareness of and connection with the true self and the Divine, we are able to clear the rubbish from our mind and our heart.

Another way of enhancing this process is to switch at least some of our focus away from ourselves and give to others some of the respect, care and attention that we feel we need. It is said that in giving we receive.

The more we take account of, and respond to, the needs of others in a positive and supportive way, the more we will grow inside and become the person we would like to be. The more we use our resources (time, mental and physical energy and money) in a worthwhile way for the benefit of others, as well as ourselves, the less depressed we are likely to be.

The mind cannot focus on two things at once. It's either *me or we.*

So if we want more love in our life, we need to give love to others. If we want other people's time and attention, we need to give ours to them. If we want to be happy, we must do our best to make others happy.

To begin with this might feel rather challenging but we can 'fake it until we make it'. Our good intentions for others will eventually bear fruit and we will go beyond depression, stress and anxiety into a better, more supportive and caring place. Shining our light in this way will encourage others to shine their light too. One day we will all shine together!

PAUSE FOR THOUGHT

- What do you need most from other people at this moment in time?
- How can you create more of this in your life?

SUMMARY

The Divine can give us the strength, support and power to deal with depression provided we open our mind and heart and ask for it.

The Divine connection has to be discovered and explored in our own way and in our own time. It is not a matter of blind faith, or accepting the dictates of others. It is a personal spiritual relationship, which can and will develop through our own unique personal experiences. However, it does require some degree of commitment, determination, courage, curiosity, honesty and humility.

By connecting and communicating with the One in whatever way we feel comfortable e.g. prayer, meditation, chanting, writing or speaking, we can overcome depression, or any other condition that is affecting our peace of mind.

CONCLUSION

We have been on a four-step journey to the core of our being.

We have explored the connection between the mind and the body and the impact that thoughts have on our mental health.

We have appreciated the benefits of creating positive thoughts and going deeper inside to reconnect with our truth and with the Divine.

We now know that we can choose to see depression, anxiety and stress as a 'wake-up call' to break out of the box of limited thinking and old habits that drag us down.

We can now see life as a spiritual gymnasium designed to help us find new paths to lasting happiness and contentment.

PART 2:
The Work – Daily Practices To Make Life Better

The lotus is the most beautiful flower,
whose petals open one by one.
But it will only grow in the mud.
In order to grow and gain wisdom, first you must have
the mud – the obstacles of life and its suffering.
If we are to strive as human beings to gain more wisdom,
more kindness and more compassion,
we must have the intention to grow as a lotus
and open each petal one by one.

Goldie Hawn

CHANGING OURSELVES takes time and practice, especially something like depression, which is a deeply engrained habit and way of thinking that may have developed over many years.

If we wish to change an old habit and replace it with a new one, we have to practice the new way of thinking and being for a minimum of 21 (some say 90) days.

The following reflective experiments, which are based on one or other of the insights in this book, are like *spiritual anti-depressants* or tools designed to lift our spirits by shifting our perception/mindset and releasing blocked energy.

Some therapists consider depression to be a form of energy that has become blocked in the body as a result of suppressing the fear, anxiety, guilt, shame and other negative emotions associated with adverse childhood experiences, or other personal traumas. By releasing these energies we become free and light.

The reflections are written in the first person and are designed to give a positive experience, which will eventually shift our mindset and restore our inner happiness.

The reflections are best when read aloud. They also work well when listened to - record them on your phone or ask someone to read them to you. They need to be read slowly with plenty of space between the words.

The more feeling that is put into words, the more effective they will be. It is essential to move from the 'head brain' i.e. logical, rational part of the self to the 'heart brain' i.e. the intuitive, feeling part of the self.

A thought filled with feeling is apparently 5000 times more powerful than a thought expressed without feeling.

The reflections can also be used as a source of stimulation and inquiry, especially those that ask questions. They provide food for thought and could be used as a stimulus for journaling.

As you will see, the reflections centre around dealing with depression. If you are more anxious or stressed, rather than depressed, then just amend each reflection to suit your own needs. They will work just as well.

The reflections are examples of what we can do when we look inside and face our challenges.

Please remember that it is very important that you create ways of healing and growing inside that work for you. For example, you might prefer to write a poem, paint a picture, create a collage, compose a piece of music or start a journal. Whatever is right for you will emerge. Follow your heart and intuition.

Note. It is not necessary to believe in any of the insights or assumptions in this book. The exercises will still work if you suspend your judgement and try them with an open mind. Put aside any misgivings you may have and, with a spirit of curiosity, give them a go. Imagine what your life would be like if they really did work!

HOW TO USE THE REFLECTIVE EXPERIMENTS

Sit quietly by yourself.

Reduce distractions to a minimum by turning off your phone, laptop etc.

Play some relaxing music and maybe burn a fragrant candle or some incense.

Ideally sit in the same space every day so that you begin to associate that place with feeling calm and peaceful.

Try a different reflection each day, whichever one attracts you.

Read it, feel it and imagine yourself being it for at least 5 minutes in the morning when you get up and 5 minute in the evening before you get in your bed.

Use each reflection throughout the day as an affirmation, especially when negatives thoughts come into your mind.

REFLECTIVE EXPERIMENTS

There is a part of you that is perfect and pure.
It is untouched by the less than perfect characteristics
you've acquired by living in a less than perfect world.

It is filled with divine qualities,
so is in a constant state of resourcefulness and wellbeing.
It's total absence of conflict and negativity of any sort
makes this part of you a Still Point – a deep,
enriching, experience of Silence.

Dadi Janki, *Companion of God*

I BREATHE

I focus on my breath
I breathe
Slowly
Deeply
Gently
Into my diaphragm
I fill my lungs from the bottom to the top
I hold the breath for the count of three
I slowly release the breath through my mouth
With each breath in
I imagine filling myself with a
Golden
Glowing
Gentle
Energy.
It relaxes my mind and body.
With each breath out
I let go of:
Anxiety
Fear
Distress.
Peace fills my heart and mind
I feel light and happy inside.

I RELAX

I tense and relax each part of my body
I notice the difference
Between the tensed and relaxed state of my:
Toes
Calf muscles
Thighs
Stomach muscles
Hands and arms
Shoulders
Jaw muscles (push the tongue against the roof of your mouth)
Facial muscles (screw your eyes into a tight ball)
My body is relaxed
I am calm inside
I am at peace with myself
And the world.

I CHANGE MY POSTURE

I sit upright
I uncross my arms and legs
I unclench my hands and place them on my lap
I raise my head
I relax my jaw
I gently gaze around me
I breathe deeply and slowly
I stand erect
I relax my shoulders
I walk with dignity and self-respect
I smile
All is well in my world.

I AM WELL

I see myself on the screen of my mind
As a carefree person.
My body is relaxed
There is a smile on my face
My eyes shine with delight
I feel good inside.
My mind is calm and clear.
Filled with positive energy
I walk with a spring in my step.
I am the master of myself
I feel light and free
Happy to be me.

I CONNECT

I sit in silence
I turn my attention inwards
I remember
I am a soul
Separate from but connected to this body.
I am an eternal being
I am immortal
I...am...peace
I...am...love
I...am...joy.
Happy and content
I carry these feelings with me throughout the day.

I AM PEACE

Whenever I feel low
I say to myself
I...am...a...peaceful...being
I...am...a...peaceful...being
I...am...a...peaceful...being.
I experience the depth of these words.
I feel
Calm
Secure
Safe
Detached from the drama of my life
Able to keep my cool
Able to hold onto hope
I repeat these words regularly throughout the day
They make me feel good.

I AM LIGHT

I see myself as a point of light
Situated in the centre of my forehead
Like a sparkling star.
I draw the energy of my body into this point.
I visualise rays of light
Spreading from the point
Calming my mind
Relaxing my body
Creating an aura of love around me.
My spirit rises
I feel
Safe and
Secure.
I am
Silent
Still
At peace with myself
And the world.

I STEP BACK AND OBSERVE

Knowing my true identity
I create a space between
Myself and:
The body I inhabit
The thoughts that I create
The feelings I experience
The words I speak
The actions I perform
The roles I play.
Stepping back from all these aspects of myself
I see things more clearly.
Depression is a way
Of thinking and being
I have acquired over time.
It does not belong to me.
With a feeling of relief
I let it go and
Reclaim my peace of mind.

I PUT A FULL STOP

I put a full stop to:
The noisy voices in my head
The old recordings of the past
That put me down and
Judge and criticise my every move.
You should do this
You must do that
How dare you!
Who do you think you are?
The voices of
Self-loathing
Regret and blame
Guilt and shame
That drive me insane
The dictators
And the haters
That cause me pain
With their messages
"You're not good enough".
Turning them off
Is such a relief!
My mind clears
Fear disappears.
In the here and now
I can relax at last
And just be.

I SEE DEPRESSION AS A GIFT

As the observer and silent witness of my life
I see depression in a new way.
It is a messenger
A friend.
It has come to
Awaken me
Challenge me
Test me.
It is a call to arms
A reminder that I have lost my way
I, the soul,
Welcome
Accept
Embrace
Love and
Thank
Depression for coming into my life
It is a gift to unwrap
All is well in my world.

I AM CURIOUS

I sit with my higher self
I know depression is not part of my original identity
It has come like a thief in the night
To take away my happiness
I look at it with curiosity
I converse with it
Who are you?
Where are you from?
What are you trying to tell me?
When will you leave?
I listen to the answers
I know what I must do.
I allow myself to grieve
I let the sadness flow
I let the bitterness go
I shout and scream
And release the pain.
Thank you for coming
It is now time for us to part.
Goodbye old friend
I knew you well.
Happiness returns.
All is well in my world.

I APPRECIATE MY INNER TREASURE

Connecting with my pure essence
I become aware of my
Virtues
Qualities and
Powers.
I meet and greet my eternal friends:
Peace
Love
Joy
Patience
Courage
Determination
Resilience
Forgiveness
Compassion
Tolerance
Honesty
Each is a treasure
Each a pleasure
To be valued in my life
My support through good times and bad
They take me beyond darkness
Into the Light
I feel good inside
All is well in my world.

I PRACTICE GRATITUDE*

Looking at this list I feel
Blessed
Humbled
Fortunate
Thankful
Appreciative
Loved
Nurtured
Valued
Cared for
Connected
Inspired
Positive
Hopeful.
I thank Nature and the people in the world
Who unknowingly support my life
I am grateful to be alive
Thank you life for everything.

---

*Before doing this, make a list of 5 things you are grateful for in your life. Every time you do this reflection, increase the number until you reach at least 50!

I CHOOSE TO BE HAPPY

I am the master of my mind
I have the power to choose the life I want.
I choose to:
Open my heart
Break free from the complications of the past
Conquer fear with love
Replace anger with peace
Be happy rather than sad
Give rather than take
Accept rather than blame
Forgive rather than hate
Stay focused and aware.
I choose to:
Make the most of my precious life
Be the best that I can be
Enjoy what life offers me.

I REMEMBER THE GOOD TIMES

I take control of my mind
I refuse to keep reliving
Unhappy scenes and
Memories from the past
They make me sad
And drag me down.
I put a full stop!
Instead I remember
Happier times -
Laughing
Sharing
Caring
Playing
Loving.
I remember the people who have been kind to me.
I focus my attention on precious moments
I relax and enjoy reliving them
Knowing there are more to come!

I LET GO OF THE PAST

As a being of peace and love
I let go of all
Guilt
Anger
Shame
Blame
Humiliation and
Pain
With compassion and understanding
I release the ball and chain of my past.
I drop the heavy bags and burdens
I have been carrying for so long.
The lessons have been learned.
The debt has been paid.
I am
Happy
Care-free
Ready to move on.

I DROP THE CLOAK OF DEPRESSION

Depression is like a black cloak that surrounds me.
Dark and heavy
It weighs me down.
With courage
And love
I untie the cloak
And drop it to the ground.
With hope in my heart
I gently step away.
Light and free
I look forward to a brighter future.
All is well
All will be well.

I GO BEYOND

I, the soul, helicopter over the scenes of my life.
Seen from above and beyond the drama
I understand more clearly what has been going on.
I have survived
The ins and outs of karma
Good times and bad
Happiness and sorrow
Victory and defeat
Love and separation
Ecstasy and trauma.
Now I rise and thrive
In a union of perfect Love
In a place of rest and peace
Beyond the battlefield.
Refreshed and restored
I return to play my part
Knowing that all is as it's meant to be.

I WATCH THE DARKNESS GO

Sitting in the sanctuary of a calm and peaceful mind
I see depression as a dark cloud
Standing before me.
I gently push it away.
Moving into the distance
Becoming ever smaller
I project feelings of love onto it
And watch it disappear.
My spirits rise
Hope returns
I am free – at last.

I EMBRACE THE PAIN

Depression is a part of me
That has been suppressed and
Hidden for too long.
Knowing this
I treat it as a friend.
I welcome it into my mind.
I give it colour, shape and name.
I treat it with respect
I listen to its message
I learn the lessons.
With compassion and understanding
I accept and embrace the pain.
It dissolves.
No longer fighting with myself
I feel whole and complete again.

I LISTEN TO MY HEART

Deep inside there is a part of me
That is ancient and wise.
It knows me better than I know myself.
This gentle loving presence
Knows what's best for me.
In the silence of my mind
It whispers words of hope.
It gently guides me
Gives me insights and inspirations
Opens doors and opportunities
Points me in the right direction
Leads me safely to my destination.
All I have to do is listen
And follow it's suggestions.

I OPEN MY THIRD EYE

Beneath the debris of my life
I know I am a good soul
I have mercy on myself
I connect with my goodness
I am loving and loveable
I am kind and caring
I am unique and valuable
I have something special to give to the world.
The darkness of ignorance disappears.
There is light at the end of the tunnel
The bottomless pit of despair has a ladder I can climb
The dark clouds move away
To reveal the Sun, which is always there.
I connect with the Light
I bathe in the Light
I become light
I am light.
All is well in my world.

I ALIGN WITH THE DIVINE

I look inside myself.
With a peaceful mind
I tune into the energy of the Divine.
I bask in vibrations of unconditional love.
Feeling secure
I unlock the door of my broken heart.
It opens like a flower.
The fragrance of love spreads through and all around me
It restores my sense of wellbeing.
I feel love
I am love
I give love
To myself and others
All is well in my world.

I SIT IN THE PRESENCE OF THE DIVINE

Tuning into my spiritual essence
I sit in the presence of the Divine
The Comforter of Hearts
Love fills my being.
Without judgement
I allow the hurt and pain
From the past to come before me.
Like a silent movie
I watch it come and go.
Feelings are dissolved
Issues are resolved
I feel absolved
Whole and free
Content to be.

I SURRENDER TO GOD'S HEALING POWER

I do my best to shift the darkness
Then surrender the rest.
God's healing power
Restores my faith
Replenishes my energy
Repairs my heart
Renovates my mind
Removes my pain
Releases blocked energy
Resolves my issues
Returns me to a state of peace
Reconnects me to the world.

SUMMARY

All the above reflective experiments are designed to release us from the pain of depression, anxiety or stress and reunite us with the truth of who we really are. Knowing this we can then connect with the Divine and receive the love, support and power to restore our peace of mind and happiness.

I hope you have enjoyed them and that they will make a difference in your life.

CONCLUSION

Depression is a scourge of our time. It causes great sorrow not only to those of us who are depressed but also to those who know and love us. We can choose to dull the pain by taking mind-altering substances, like tranquillisers and alcohol, but such solutions bring only temporary relief.

If we do what we have always done, we cannot change.

If we wish to heal and overcome our depression, anxiety or stress then we need to try something new.

Spirituality offers a powerful antidote to such states of mind for those who are open to exploring their inner world. It can reboot our internal power and put us back in charge of our life so that we can create a happier future for ourselves.

I hope the insights and suggestions offered in this book will open up doors of healing and hope for you and restore your peace of mind.

May the Force be with you!

Appendix 1:
ABOUT BRAHMA KUMARIS

The Brahma Kumaris is a network of organisations in over 100 countries, with its spiritual headquarters in Mount Abu, India. The university works at all levels of society for positive change.

Acknowledging the intrinsic worth and goodness of the inner self, the University teaches a practical method of meditation that helps people to cultivate their inner strength and values.

The University also offers courses and seminars in such topics as positive thinking, overcoming anger, stress relief and self-esteem, encouraging spirituality in daily life. This spiritual approach is also brought into healthcare, social work, education, prisons and other community settings.

The University's Academy in Mount Abu, Rajasthan, India, offers individuals from all backgrounds a variety of life-long learning opportunities to help them recognize their inherent qualities and abilities in order to make the most of their lives.

All courses and activities are offered free of charge.

For more information: www.brahmakumaris.org

For Brahma Kumaris publications: www.inspiredstillnes.com

Appendix 2: ADVERSE CHILDHOOD EXPERIENCES (A.C.E.)

The impact of adverse childhood experiences on the mental and physical health of adults is now widely recognized thanks to research which started at the Kaiser Permanente's obesity clinic in San Diego, California, where staff sought to explain why 50% of participants dropped out of their weight reduction programmes.

Researchers asked over 17,000 Kaiser Permanente volunteer patients about different types of childhood trauma that had been identified in earlier research literature, namely:

- Physical abuse
- Sexual abuse
- Emotional abuse
- Physical neglect
- Emotional neglect
- Exposure to domestic violence
- Household substance abuse
- Household mental illness
- Parental separation or divorce
- Incarcerated household member

They discovered that the number of ACEs experienced by an individual was strongly associated with adulthood high-risk health behaviours such as smoking, alcohol and drug abuse, promiscuity and severe obesity and correlated with ill-health including depression, heart disease, cancer, chronic lung disease and shortened lifespan.

Compared to an ACE score of zero, having four adverse childhood experiences was associated with:

- A seven-fold (700%) increase in alcoholism
- A doubling of risk of being diagnosed with cancer
- A four-fold increase in emphysema.

An ACE score above six was associated with a 30-fold (3000%) increase in attempted suicide.

Source: Wikipedia

INSIGHTFUL BOOKS TO HELP SHIFT THE DARKNESS

Acton Smith, Michael	*Calm*, Penguin
Alcoe, Jan	*Lifting Your Spirits*, The Janki Foundation For Health Care
Arora, Neeraj	*Depression Under Cover*, Guildford Press
Ben-Shahar, Tal	*Happier*, McGraw Hill
Brotheridge, Chloe	*The Anxiety Solution*, Penguin
Cotton, Fearne	*Quiet*, Orion Spring
Covey, Stephen	*7 Habits of Highly Effective People*, Simon & Schuster
De Seriere, Annemarie	*Will To Wonder*, Annemarie De Seriere
Field, Lynda	*60 Tips For Self-Esteem*, Element
Frankel, Viktor	*Man's Search For Meaning*, Rider
George, Mike	*Discover Inner Peace*, Duncan Baird
George, Mike	*The 7 Aha's of Highly Enlightened Souls*, O Books
Haig, Matt	*Reasons To Stay Alive*, Canongate Books

Hamilton, David — *The Five Effects of Kindness*, Hay House UK

Hay, Louise L. — *You Can Heal Your Life*, Hay House

Holden, Robert — *Shift Happiness*, Hodder & Stoughton

Janki, Dadi — *Companion of God*, BKIS

Janki, Dadi — *The Gift Of Peace*, BKIS

Lipton, Bruce — *The Biology of Belief*, Hay House

Katie, Byron — *Loving What Is*, Rider

Kirpalani, Jayanti — *God's Healing Power*, Penguin

Kirpalani, Jayanti — *The Power of Meditation*, BKIS

Ladva, Aruna — *It's Time to Be Cool*, BKIS

Lindfield, Gael — *The Emotional Healing Strategy*, Penguin

Moorjani, Anita — *Dying To Be Me*, Hay House

Murray, Joseph — *The Power of Your Subconscious*, Pocket Books

Neff, Kristen — *Self Compassion*, Hodder & Stoughton

Nelson, Bradley — *The Emotion Code*, Wellness Unmasked Publishing

Peck, Scott M — *Further Along The Road Less Travelled*, Pocket Books

Richardson, Cheryl — *The Art of Extreme Self Care,* Hay House

Rowe, Dorothy — *The Courage To Live*, Fontana

Ruskan, John — *Emotional Clearing*, Rider

Servan, David — *Healing Without Freud or Prozac,* Rodale

Smith, David Miln — *Hug The Monster*, Rider

Swan, Teal — *Anatomy of Loneliness*, Watkins

Taylor, Steve — *The Fall*, Iff Books

Tolle, Eckhart — *The Power of Now,* Yellow Kite

Topham, Sally — *Finding The River,* Dragon Rising Publishing

Tracey, Brian — *Change Your Thinking, Change Your Life.* Hodder Mobius

Verma, Shivani — *Happiness Unlimited*, Amaryllis

Wax, Ruby — *Sane New World*, Hodder & Stoughton

Williams, Mark — *The Mindful Way Through Depression*, Guildford Press

Williams, Nick — *Unconditional Success*, Bantam Books

APPS TO KEEP YOU CALM AND LIFT YOUR SPIRITS

BeeZone
Provides a variety of free tools to enable you to take a break from a racing, stressful mind and come back to calmness and focus. It can be used by anyone.

Calm
Helps users to sleep better, boost their confidence and reduce stress and anxiety, with the help of guided meditations, soothing music and bedtime stories.

Happidote
A free app specially designed to assist healthcare professionals. Happidote (think happy antidote!) offers an easy way to access practical advice through guided meditations to help calm your mind and soothe the stress of work.

Happiful
Gives free access to the Happiful monthly magazine which promotes positive mental health and gives access to a directory of therapies, therapists and wellbeing courses.

Headspace
Teaches the life-changing skills of meditation and mindfulness in just a few minutes a day - through hundreds of guided sessions on everything from managing stress and anxiety to sleep, productivity, exercise and physical health.

Just-a-minute
Experience the power of a quiet mind with forty one-minute relaxing meditations to transform your day. Free of charge.

Meditation Lounge
A variety of meditations based on raja yoga to help with a bad day, a tricky relationship, a frazzling deadline. Or just to relax and find some peace of mind. Free of charge.

Radio Eyesee
Plays soft music for meditation, reflection and relaxation day and night with weekly randomising of tracks.

YouTube
Has lots of beautiful meditation music freely available to calm you down and lift you up.

MENTAL HEALTH CHARITIES (UK) OFFERING SUPPORT/ADVICE

Here is a selection of some of the charities in the UK offering mental health support. Similar organisations exist In other countries.

Beat (www.beateatingdisorders.org.uk)
Supports anyone who may be dealing with an eating disorder.

Calm (www.thecalmzone.net)
Campaign Against Living Miserably offers confidential and free support to men anywhere in the UK through a helpline and a webchat service.

Mind (www.mind.org.uk)
Provides advice and support to empower anyone experiencing a mental health problem .

Mental Health Foundation (www.mentalhealth.org.uk)
Dedicated to the prevention of mental health through research and campaigns.

Ocdaction (www.ocdaction.org.uk)
Campaigns for better treatment and can provide specific advice on how to overcome your OCD (obsessive compulsive disorder).

Samaritans (www.samaritans.org)
Provides round the clock telephone support for people who are struggling and needing to talk.

Shout (www.giveusashout.org)
Offers a round the clock text messaging service for anyone in need of support.Text to Shout 85258

The Mix (www.themix.org.uk)
Offers support to under 25s via phone, email or webchat.

Together (www.together-uk.org)
Supports people through mental health services.

Young Minds (www.youngminds.org.uk)
Supports and empowers young people and their parents.

ACKNOWLEDGEMENTS

First and foremost I would like to thank Dadi Janki, former Administrative Head of Brahma Kumaris, Jayanti Kirpalani, Maureen Goodman, other teachers and friends at Brahma Kumaris. The knowledge, understanding and commitment of the organisation to changing human consciousness is amazing. It has completely changed my life.

Thanks also to the support and encouragement of Judy Apps, Judy Johnson, Nick Williams, Jan Alcoe, Doug Stephenson, who kindly edited the book, Georgina Long, Sarah Eagger, Kala Mistry, Jaymini Patel, Marion Ngai, Phillipa Blackham, Georgeanne Lamont, Madhvi Lamba, Diane Tillman, Neville Hodgkinson, Mike George, Marguerite Byrne, Jim Ryan, Liz Corrigan, Margaret McCathie, Josephine Occloo, Arnold Desser, Firoz Hussein, Nina Buchanan, Jonathan Jones, Mai Newe, Tom Costley, Bicky Saika, Patrik Somers-Stephenson, Caroline Ward, Shaan Sampat. Not forgetting my son, daughter and brother, who gave me the occasional necessary prod!

Finally, thanks to the One for the knowledge and support that has made this book possible.

ABOUT THE AUTHOR

John McConnel is a speaker, trainer, workshop facilitator, spiritual teacher and writer who lives in London. He has worked as a prison governor, social worker and stress management trainer and helped many depressed and stressed people in his life, including himself!

John has been studying and teaching raja yoga meditation for nearly 30 years. He has a strong interest in the practical application of spiritual principles and insights in daily life and conducts seminars in the UK and abroad on a variety of personal development topics with a view to enabling people to improve the quality of their life and so help change the world.

He believes that returning to an inner state of peace and happiness is the single most important thing that we can do in these troubled times.

Contact him at info@stresslesstraining.co.uk

Printed in Poland
by Amazon Fulfillment
Poland Sp. z o.o., Wrocław

56724769R00094